When the Wind Blows and the Sun Shines

Based on an Aesop Fable

Retold by Alison Hawes
Illustrated by Bee Willey

Rigby®
A Harcourt Achieve Imprint

www.Rigby.com
1-800-531-5015

The wind and the sun were talking.
The wind said to the sun,
"I am stronger than you."

2

"No," said the sun,
"*I* am stronger than *you*."

3

"Do you see that man down there?" said the wind.

4

The sun looked down.
There was a man walking across a field.
"Yes, I see him," said the sun.

5

"I will get the man
to take his coat off first,"
said the wind.

6

"No," said the sun,
"*I* will get him to take his coat off first."

"We will see," said the wind.

The wind went first.
It blew and blew.

8

The man felt the wind on his back.
"The wind *is* strong," he said,
pulling his coat to him.

Again, the wind blew and blew and BLEW!

10

Again, the man felt the wind on his back.
"The wind is *very* strong," he said,
pulling his coat to him again.

"I will try now,"
said the sun.
It shone and shone.

12

The man felt the sun on his back.
"The sun *is* strong," he said,
pushing back his coat.

13

Again, the sun shone and shone and SHONE!

14

Again, the man felt the sun on his back.
"The sun is *very* strong," he said,
taking off his coat.
"It is going to be a good day."

"There," said the smiling sun.
"I *am* stronger than you!"
And the wind was so angry
that it blew away to sea.

16